Another Day
Called Tomorrow

Patricia Harris

DEDICATION

In memory of my wonderful husband Derek who went to
be with the Lord 18th July 2020 and with whom I shared
the adventures in this book

CONTENTS

FOREWORD

I am privileged to write this foreword for Pat's book 'Another Day Called Tomorrow'.

Derek has been my long time friend and he and Pat together made zealous efforts to help alleviate the plight of the children who from early childhood were forced to live in State orphanages in Romania.

After the collapse of the communist regime the church of which I was the minister along with many others, sent teams to assist.

Derek and Pat were in the vanguard of the mission and what they saw inspired them to do all they could to alert and inspire others to take up the challenge to try to improve the appalling conditions.

They pioneered the funding of our children's home 'Karisma' and encouraged many people to subscribe to the purchase of the property which was refurbished and extended and became a home to a number of young people who were given hope for their future.

There must be many people in Romania now who can look back and gratefully remember an English couple, Derek and Pat.

Rev. Gordon Bates. Retired minister of Thundersley Congregational Church.

The orphanage was quiet.......are there no children here?   But yes at orphanage one there were little babies with blank eyes laying in dirty cots, or quietly rocking back and forth.

At orphanage two the older children wandered listlessly around the room or lay in cots far too small for them.

Or little faces were pressed against the windows looking and waiting for the Mama who never came for them!

These are the words of one of these children, written as an adult " All I dreamt of was another day called tomorrow!   And hoped it would be a better day.

PREFACE

I woke one night in early December 1989 with the thought on my mind 'pray for the people of Romania'. So I did, I had no idea why, I didn't know a thing about the country and hadn't any desire to learn about it before that. I didn't have long to find out that our lives as well as the people of that country was about to change.

I met Derek in 1986 and by 1987 God had shown us that we were to have a life together. In 1988 we married. In Dereks words "Life is an adventure with you!" And so our life together with God began. The following are accounts of some of these adventures in Romania beginning in 1990.............

Derek and I had been married for about eighteen months when we both felt that we would like to be involved in some sort of mission work, most likely with children. Derek had been made redundant and took early retirement just three weeks after we married. By rearranging some of my community nursing shifts I was able to take several weeks of extended holiday.

Our church had been involved with YWAM (Youth With A Mission) and there was an opportunity to join a project for some children's work in Uganda. We joined a team and met with them several times during the latter months of 1989, with the idea that the project would go ahead during the summer of 1990. However we were told that this was not likely to happen for a while, and the choice was either to wait until later, or see if there was something else with children that God wanted us to be involved with. The rest of the team wanted to wait. Derek and I felt that God was calling us to do something now…….. but what?

We didn't have too long to wait. The news programmes on television after the Romanian revolution showed the world the pitiful plight of the children living in the orphanages, and the aid that was needed to help the people of that country also......

We were invited to join a team that was going to Romania that summer and we both felt that this was the right thing for us. We went to meet the rest of the team and to learn about the Romanian culture. There were all sorts of do's and don'ts to learn about relating to mission.........

And so the adventure began..........

We believed it would be for just one visit but stopped counting in 2000 when we had been at least twenty plus times. Sometimes we went for for two or three weeks at a time with occasional three month stays.

****

In the middle of November 1989 the Berlin wall fell! It was the beginning of unrest in communist countries.

Romania had been under Communist rule for 42 years and the revolution started there in Timisoara on 16th December 1989.. It spread to many cities with hundreds of people being killed, ending on 25th December 1989 when the dictator Nicolae Ceaucescu and his wife Elena were executed by the people......... And so the country was opened up to the world to see the devastating effects on the people and the country and a new life for them began.........

THE ADVENTURE BEGINS

The day of our first visit to Romania had arrived. We met the rest of the YWAM team at the airport only to be told that our flight would be delayed. After a few hours we took off in a very old Tarot aeroplane (Tarom was the Romanian state airline). Tarom aeroplanes at that time were very basic, the seats were just bolted down so that the plane could revert to military very quickly if needed.

We were served a meal which was quite tasty. We ate hungrily and our flight time passed anticipating what lay ahead!

Bucuresti Airport terminal building at that time was little more than a shack; we really felt we had gone back in time! Waiting for us was our host Emil, who greeted us very warmly; it seemed he had great difficulty containing his excitement at meeting us. (The Baptist church in Bucuresti had been asked for families to host the visiting teams). Emil had been waiting for us for four hours in extreme heat! His English was good and he told us we were to travel into the city from the airport by tram, being some miles from the apartment where he lived.

Emil and his family lived on the twelfth floor of one of the many apartment blocks which all looked identical.

The stairwells were dark with just a single light bulb every couple of floors and the lift wasn't working. Emil's wife Rodica and their five children were at the door to welcome us with open arms.

By this time it was midnight but waiting for us on the table was a feast, salata de boeuf and cozanac, so we tucked in and had a little chat with the family with Emil who was very good at interpreting. We were extremely tired and glad to be able to get to bed.

Derek and I were given one room and the rest of the family bedded down in the other bedroom and living room.

Before long my tummy was gurgling and I had to rush to the toilet. Whatever I had eaten on the plane, had left Romania in the morning, gone to England and then we ate it on board on the return journey. There was no fridge on board and with 30 degree summer heat it no doubt had developed a few bugs before I ate it and my tummy was complaining.

After I had spent an hour or so in the only bathroom I could hear the desperate little voices of the children waiting to use it before they went to school and I believe they had to go to use a neighbours first!

So Romania for us felt very strange and I'm sure the family's introduction to us was very strange for them also! However this family were to become a much loved part of our lives, although we didn't know that at the time.

ORPHANAGES - FIRST IMPRESSIONS

There were more than 100,000 Romanian children in orphanages by the end of 1989 when communism ended. When the dictator Nicolae Ceaucescu was overthrown in 1989 Romania was opened up to the world for the first time.

When he took power in 1965 there was a declining birthrate, so he instituted policies banning abortion, restricting divorce and instituting a childlessness tax, and so many children entered orphanages as parents were unable to cope with their growing families. The state stepped in stating that it could do a better job than the parents in raising the children. The belief that this was right paired with the dire economic climate meant many parents were left with little means to look after their children. The conditions in the orphanages deteriorated and many were treated appallingly. Many of these children were not truly orphans which I suppose was reflected in the name Leaganul which roughly translated meant swing facility   where these children 'swung ' from one institution to another according to age.   They mainly were children abandoned by their parents because they couldn't afford to keep them or because of some disability or illness.

On the first day, our introduction to the orphanage seemed a little different to the scenes that we had seen on the television news in England. The director of the orphanage and a few well dressed ladies were there to great us. Then we were taken into a room and introduced to a few of the children; they were dressed reasonably well and there were toys there too…something seemed odd about the toys then we realised that they were not able to be played with as they were either hung from the ceiling or stuck on the walls, so the children couldn't play with anything!

Later we discovered that the picture we were first given was to try to get visitors to see things differently to the reality that we soon would find.

The next day it was a little different when they understood that we were there to stay for longer and we then got to see the true situation of how the children were treated.

Outside leaganul doi (orphanage No. 2)

There were two orphanages that we were to become involved with, number one was where the babies and children up to the age of about two lived......they were left in their cots most of the day.   There were row on row of cots with only inches between them and in awful condition; the metal parts rusty, the mattresses lumpy and very dirty and unhygienic.

The children, if they were able to stand, were wearing an all in one piece of clothing that had feet so that when the children soiled themselves the poo would just drop into the feet part and wouldn't come out   in the cots.   The babies   didn't have   nappies but just rags tied around their waists. They were covered   in spots and we wondered what had caused them. We discovered that they were actually bedbug bites. When we went in at night, if the lights were switched on suddenly, the children and the beds would be black with the bugs.

On subsequent visits we were able to take new cots and mattresses that had been donated from England.

At the number two orphanage where the older children lived, many of them were damaged mentally because of being abandoned as babies and left in cots all day with no love or stimulation.and these children were classed as 'defective'.

Many would just rock back and forth all day. During our time there much of it was spent just picking the children up and cuddling them and trying to show them some love, playing with them and getting them to play too. On later visits we took clothing and toys, colouring and painting supplies and things that would stimulate the children.

We taught them songs in English and learned a few in Romanian.

We liaised with the director of the orphanage to see what improvements we could do on future visits to help make their lives better and so were asked to rebuild some of the areas in the garden that would make it better and easier for the children to be able to play outside. We also were asked to take down walls in the orphanage to make a bigger space so that the children weren't separated from each other and would be able to play together.

We came came home from our first visit to Romania our lives changed forever, but little did we know what lay ahead……

THE MAN ON THE RADIO

We discovered on our first visit that there was a shortage of water everywhere, as all water was supplied to the buildings by the state, and so during the main working day the water supply to homes, including the orphanages was redirected to factories.

It was very difficult for everyone especially during the very hot summer weather with no water to drink or cook with and so enough had to be stored in pots and pans for the day. Also in the orphanage there was no hot water either, which meant that the children were often dumped in freezing baths (the water came from the mountains above Focsani). Sometimes the same water was used for bathing several children, one after another, often cleaning off bodily waste, and so disease spread between the children.

We told of our experiences when we got back and the need for water.... perhaps we could supply and install a water storage system......?

No sooner said than the pastor of our church announced to the congregation that we would be returning in the October - just three months later - with a team to do just that. But how was this to come about? We knew little about the practicalities of this and so we prayed 'Lord if this is really what you want us to do you will have to show us how'!

The very next day I was listening to the local radio station and heard an interview with a man who had just returned from Romania having taken a team to install a water storage system in an orphanage! Now this man would be able to help and give us much needed information!

I phoned the radio station to see if they could put me in touch with him, 'no' they said. They really didn't know who he was or how to find him. Well I thought we had asked God to show us and this was the answer - but perhaps not?

However at that time I was nursing in the community and many of my patients were interested in what we were doing, especially as there had been so much about it on the news in recent days.

One morning I was greeted with great excitement by the wife of my patient. She had been at the fracture clinic at our local hospital with her grandson. As she sat there waiting she got chatting to the man next to her who had his leg in plaster, he told her he had broken it falling down an open manhole in Romania, where he had been installing a water storage system in an orphanage! Wow, he was our man from the radio and she was able to get his telephone number!!
Coincidence? No another God-incidence of which we had many.

We made contact with him and he was able to give us a lot of useful information and advice.

Derek and another man flew out to Romania in the September to see if it was practical for us to do this and get permission from the local mayor. (Mayors had major influence over all aspects of their towns and villages and it was the practice for them to give their approval) And so in the October we set off by road with three Luton vans full of all the donated equipment that we needed to carry out this work.

PIGEON STEW AND DOCK LEAF SOUP

R omanian folk were so generous with the food that they had, and would give us food even if they didn't have any themselves. They would serve us food and watch us eat and then if there was any left they would have that themselves. Mamaliga was a favourite which was made with corn meal and often was eaten with sour cream or a type of cheese called branza.

We didn't always ask what we were eating, but on occasions we discovered for ourselves that the food was quite different to anything we would eat in England. Romanians were often very resourceful using all kinds of different plants. One lady had given us a sort of pigeon stew (the pigeon she had caught from the roof that morning!) this was okay until we sat opposite her as she was eating the bones of the pigeon and crunching them loudly! Most days there was soup and on one occasion when we asked what it was, were told 'see that plant over there' which was dock leaf, so discovered we were eating dock leaf soup.

Some time later when we were staying for an extended time in Focsani we were shopping, buying and cooking our own food and there were queues at the market for the fresh foods. I remember on one occasion feeling very guilty as I had just bought some nice pieces of chicken and was standing next to a man who was buying chicken beaks and feet and realised that that was all he could afford to make soup with to feed his children. There were many families living like that.

We were warned on our first visit there never to buy or eat anything from the street, but the heat being extreme we were very thirsty and so we bought a bottle of fruit juice. When we got back to the hotel where we were staying it had been standing for a while. I went to pick it up to have a drink; at that point the top flew off and the entire contents emptied itself all over the wall and ceiling of the hotel bedroom, but we felt very fortunate that we hadn't actually drunk any of it.

On our first visit to the orphanage in Focsani I was still feeling quite ill from eating the food on the plane and I had spent one day in bed at the hotel. One of the doctors from the orphanage came and delivered some antibiotics for me and I was told to take sixteen pills in one go! She brought me some stewed apples with lots of sugar and said it would help me to get better!

Later after several visits I was very wary about having to go to hospital if I needed help, having seen some first hand, so on another visit there when I twisted my ankle as I stepped off the pavement I was reluctant to seek hospital help. My ankle swelled up and I couldn't walk. Someone came in a car to get me and take me back to our apartment, where our host's mother massaged the enormous lump that had come up on my foot which helped to reduce it, but it was several days before I could walk on it properly and I had to hobble along with a stick.

WOW - HOT WATER AT LAST!

In October of 1990 we set out with three Luton vans full of the equipment needed to install the water storage system in the orphanage at Focsani. There were six men and myself. We travelled through France, Belgium, Germany, Austria, Hungary and finally reached Romania. It was a three day journey with many adventures on the way - maybe time for some of those later!

We had only a week there to install the complete system and get it up and working. The men started work early in the morning and continued during the afternoon siesta time. In the evening we ate together with the orphanage staff and they would organise some Romanian dancing or other activity that we quite enjoyed even though really tired.by this time.

I spent my days helping with the children, getting to know the staff and hoping that they would accept me as a

Installing the water storage system

Installing the water storage system

friend who wanted to help. There were many requests for help as so many people were suffering at that time.

The installation went well with the Romanian maintenance man from the orphanage watching what the men were doing. He would occasionally give advice about which pipes were the right ones to connect to. However on the last day everything was in place and with baited breath the team were ready to try it out.......The discovery was then made that the maintenance man had deliberately given them misleading information so everything had been connected up wrongly.

Oh no......our timing was very tight as we had another three day journey back across Europe to get our ferry home, most of our team having to be back at work in England with no extra time to spare,

Perhaps this could be done somehow in the one day that we had allowed in case of difficulties journeying. The next morning we were all up early to try to reconnect the pipes correctly.

****

During that morning our interpreter Lulu came to say that there was a very agitated priest who wanted to see us and take us for a meal. We said that was not possible as the work had to be completed that day. However, Lulu was insistent that we must go, so Derek and I and one other man left the other four to get finished and went off to meet this agitated priest!

I looked out of the window and saw a man pacing up and down and really didn't want to go. Why would we want to meet this man? However, once again when we responded we realised that this was all part of God's plan for us in that place, and another chapter opened.

Valentin Ghica wasn't an agitated priest but was the 'very anxious to meet us' pastor of the Brethren church in Focsani. He and his wife Aneta and their five children were to become great friends and so much part of our lives there in Romania.

He had many tales to tell of the persecution and interrogation by the Securitate especially as Christians, and we listened to the stories and understood a little more of life under the communist regime and the wicked dictator Nicolae Ceacescu.

Fear was all around us still, so much mistrust and even though we were accepted as Christian brothers and sisters, they couldn't quite let themselves believe that we were ok.

We were staying in the one and only hotel in Focsani, very hard to describe as a hotel! The bedding was lumpy and uncomfortable and the sheets looked as though they had seen better days. The towels were threadbare and you certainly wouldn't want to have one in your home, but in spite of that we were accused of stealing one!

On one occasion when at Pastor Ghica's home (whom we were later to affectionately call P G) he called a taxi for us to take us back to the hotel and we went on a half hour journey to get there.

It was only on subsequent visits that we found that the hotel was actually only over the road, a two minute walk away, but he didn't want us to know at that time where he and his family lived! Such was the fear and suspicion that they lived with.

REVOLUTION AFTERMATH

The effects of communism still had its effect for many years in Romania and you could sense the distrust and suspicion of foreigners.

The family we first stayed with went very quiet if there was a knock at the door and they would be very wary who would be there, especially as until we had come, there was no way that they would have been allowed to have any Westerners in their homes. We were somewhat of a novelty at that time and many people came to see us.

The Romanian Orthodox Church was the main Christian organisation which was recognised and controlled by the state. Many Christians were persecuted for their faith. Richard Wurmbrand was a Romanian Christian pastor who was imprisoned and tortured for his faith. He was kept in isolation in dark underground cells for many years. We heard many stories from the Christians there of persecution and hardship because of their faith. Even after the country opened up to the outside world we had to have our visas renewed and the police would check our address during our longer stays in Romania.

When we first went In 1990 we met many people who had been involved in the revolution, the bullet scarred walls were there for us all to see and made the reality of the revolution come alive, especially when we met some of the people who had been involved.

We met a lovely family - a mother and her two little girls. The father had been amongst those protesting on the streets. He had been shot and taken to hospital where the Securitate had come and found him and then shot and killed him in his hospital bed! The family were left fatherless with no one to support them.

Another family that we met on our first visit in 1990 was a family of five children. The parents were Mimi and

Gigi. The youngest child was a little girl called Delia.

Delia was completely paralysed and brain damaged due to an accident. The family lived in a second floor apartment and the child had crawled out onto the landing and fallen through a gap in the guard rails to the floor two storeys below. They were such a loving family, there was no help for their disabled child and they devoted themselves to caring for her. During the years that followed we visited them every time we were in Bucuresti. She was unable to do anything for herself and her brothers and sister helped with the caring. We learnt just recently (2020) that this little girl, now a thirty two year old woman, died a few months ago.

On our first stay in this country, shortly after the revolution, shelves in the shops were bare, maybe just one or two kinds of tins on empty shelves. The people queued for hours waiting for food deliveries, not knowing what was going to be delivered next. Sometimes they waited many hours in the queue, occasionally leaving for a short time and reserving their place by putting a shopping bag down on the ground. After waiting they were pleased to get whatever was delivered, maybe sugar, maybe butter. Food parcels from other countries helped them to survive. It was wonderful to see Emil's reactions to the different things that they had never seen before. We had some tins of shark once which was a bit leathery, but they would share whatever they had with us and we had wonderful Romanian meals that we had never had before, that we came to really enjoy over the years.

Emil was such a lovely caring man and it was a delight to see the happiness that it gave him as he shared what he had been given, often taking things to someone who he felt was more needy. We once took him a pair of shoes as the only ones that he had were much too big for him and so he had them stuffed with newspaper to keep them from falling off, but he took the ones that we gave him to a neighbour on the floor above him who didn't have any shoes at all.

Emil also delighted in showing us the sites around the city, but it was only later when we tried to find our own way around and couldn't find the places that he had shown us that we realised Emil loved to translate names into English. So when he told us "this is Stephen the Great" it was actually Stefan cel Mare! We went to a place in the countryside that was called Campulung but he actually told us the English translation which was Longfield!

We brought Emil, Rodica and their eldest two children to England for a holiday that first Christmas in 1990. Everything in England was such a wonder to them and when we took them to a Tesco superstore, their eyes wide open with awe, they were taking photos of the food saying that there was more food in the store than in the entire city of Bucuresti!

We didn't realise that summer when we invited them to come for Christmas, that Rodica was already pregnant with her sixth child. There was an airport strike in the January and so their flight home was delayed.   Just three weeks after their return home they had a little daughter (they named her Patricia after me) who is now married herself with her own little baby.

During the communist era whole villages and peoples homes had been destroyed by Nicolai Ceaucescu and his wife, the people had been brought into the cities and housed in tower blocks, their land taken from them.

Amongst the many shortages it was extremely difficult to get light bulbs and they had become very precious. One family we knew had only one light bulb for the entire apartment and it was taken from room to room as and when it was needed.

The stairwells in the tower blocks had only one light every few floors, and no windows so it was a matter of feeling your way up and down and hoping that you didn't slip and fall. The stairs were not of equal size and depth so they were quite dangerous to navigate even with light, but in the dark it was very precarious when feet are used to stairs being regular sizes. Also many times there were no lights in the lifts either.

Once when we were getting into the lift with my torch I managed to press floor level twelve before the lift door closed and handed the torch out to the friends that were waiting for it to come back down to them. I must say that it was quite scary travelling in that pitch dark lift and hoping it would reach the floor that you wanted and that there would be some light to be able to see as you got out!

Hospitals fared no better in their need for light......we heard of a doctor who had gone to get into a lift, but with no lights had not been able to see that although the door was open the lift wasn't there, and so he stepped in and plunged to his death.

As already mentioned Emil and Rodica lived on the twelfth floor of a tower block and occasionally the lift was not working at all and you had to walk up and down.. When it was working, sometimes it would stop between floors, once stopping half way between floor twelve and thirteen. Fortunately Emil was in the lift with us at that time and he just jumped until it gradually dropped down to floor twelve where we could get out!

Wherever we went there were so many needs, and having heard about our water storage installation at the orphanage people were asking if we could help them too.

. *Derek by a village pump*

In one village there was no running water at all just a couple of hand pump wells. So the doctor's surgery and a home for old people were desperate for us to help them.

We soon learned that we had to give a definite yes or no to requests, there was not such a thing as 'maybe', or 'we'll think and pray about it' as that was taken as a yes and we had a few angry confrontations with some people who thought that we had promised to help. Valuable lessons learned.

FRIED RAT!

After our initial visits to Romania in 1990, we returned two or three times each year taking aid and to help care for some of the children, also for the first few years taking medication for the very sick children. We were also able to equip them with new cots and mattresses. We also took teams with us for outreach over the next few years.

There were two state orphanages in Focsani, a town about 150 miles north of Bucuresti, that we were involved with.

One evening Danut (the orphanage director) was called to the orphanage as the electricity had gone off. Derek and Danut made their way there, only to find that outside in the box that held the very ancient coils for the electricity someone had left a part eaten sandwich, An enormous rat had got in and his nose and tail had touched the two coils and plunged the orphanage into darkness. The rat had burnt to a cinder!

ANOTHER DAY CALLED TOMORROW FOR JEAN

We spent many hours over the years with these lovely children.........We were there in the very very hot summers and the very very cold winters……as well as the seasons in between.

At orphanage two (Leagunal doi) the children when we first met them were between one and a half and two years old. One of the children was a little guy that we called Spikey because his hair stood up on the top of his head. The following is something that this little boy now aged 32, wrote recently.

His name is Jean and this is his story… ….(Written 2020 and translated from Romanian.)

"Wow can't believe the years have passed and I'm still in this earthly fight. Since young, God had a plan and still has for me. Even though people used to call

me Spikey when I was a kid I still didn't know who this soul was holding my hand, I thought it was Mama. But it was Pat and I didn't know who this soul was. She looked at me with so much tenderness. I was in the crib and people were visiting, I was waiting momentarily for Mom to come, but I was forgotten and abandoned, it was hard. Sometimes I leaned on the window and looked out to watch for when Mama comes to get me a home, but we were still at the orphanage! I was always getting in the crib crying and didn't know where I was. Even though I was protected from the rain and thunder, it was still me and my crib. But what helped me was that it wasn't just me, I had other friends with me in their beds. I would get up and see many kids, but I still didn't know where they were. When I heard crying I cried too, thinking not that I was protected where I was. But as the seasons came again and I grew up and I was still waiting, maybe I'll get it, someones home. But one day in 1999, ladies came from England, and offered a home to me, gave me joy to believe in love and grow beautifully. And to really find out who I am, and why I came into this world, and what was the purpose of being born and being in an orphanage. Life passed I became a teenager, I knew now who my parents are and what God did for me. It was a joy that I cannot explain in words, it was a dream. Getting out of an orphanage and having my own home, my own room. I never believed in my life that God gives me this joy. Evelyn and Ruth, made a beautiful work, a complicated but also beautiful work. God gave them the power to give us a home, a family and to know God. Growing up I was thanking them and crying and telling these moms I didn't think I would have my own room and I would have parents. I thank them so much for what they have done for me. Memories I will never forget.

(Included with permission and translated from the original Romanian text).

ALINA

We first met Alina in 1994 when she came to live at the orphanage in Focsani. Alina was to become our daughter in 1999. We had no intention of becoming adoptive parents as I was fifty four and Derek was sixty five, but God had other ideas.

Many times over the next few years when we were in Romania Alina would either come out with us or come to stay with us and we had got really close over this time.

We had been in Romania for three months from January to end of March 1998 and during, that time we had been to the authorities to see if we could bring Alina to England for a holiday. We had to undergo lots of questioning and agree to bring a chaperone to England with her.

They wanted us to bring someone from the orphanage staff as chaperone but we persuaded them that Tanta (the lady that we had been staying with) would be suitable to accompany her. So Tanta and her four year old daughter Madalina and Alina came to England for a holiday in the April for three months.

One night during that time I woke with the thought on my mind that we should adopt Alina......it seemed a ridiculous idea mainly because of our ages but also as Alina had a life threatening condition.

Was this just a thought that had come to me or should I speak to Derek about it? Next day I nervously decided that if I didn't ask Derek then I would never know if this was just me or did God really want us to do it?

Well Derek had also been thinking the same thing.   Also Alina who understood and spoke quite good English (she had taught herself from the Romanian subtitles of American films that she had seen on TV in Romania) only that day had been watching the film Cinderella and she said to me, "If I had a fairy godmother and one wish it would be that you and Daddy would be younger so that you could adopt me". She had been calling us Mummy and Daddy for some time.

Was this just a very silly thought, as I was fifty four years old and Derek was sixty five.or did God really want us to do it?   Alina's health problems might also make it difficult for us to adopt her.

Alina, Tanta and Madalina returned to Romania in July and we began to make enquiries to see if it would be a possibility.

We made some enquiries and found out that it would be very difficult to adopt but not impossible. The first thing that we had to do was to go back to Romania to find her birth mother and get her written permission for the adoption. Then we had to go through a home study in England and get passed by a panel to be approved as adoptive parents. Usually the home study took a couple of years to complete and was very costly to do this if the adoption was to be from another country.   Then we would have to go back to Romania again and do all of the legal things to be able to adopt there.

So we returned to Romania in September 1998 and managed to find Alina's mother and get her to sign the correct papers. We had intended to stay there for three months but now needed to come home to do the home study. In normal circumstances this was going to take two years and was to be very intense, where every aspect of our lives was scrutinised. Adopting from abroad was very costly as the home study meant we had to pay for the Social Worker who does the study and all of the legal fees.

The return visit to Romania was another adventure in itself………

HIGHWAY ROBBERY IN HUNGARY

A t that time in Romania there were still no banks that we could transfer money to, so all money had to be taken out with us in cash.

We once again set off on our now familiar journey through Europe to Romania. Our first stop was in Austria where we had made friends with a lovely lady in her late seventies who had a nice little guest house. The next morning we said our farewells to Frau Weber and started day two of our travel.

After arriving in Hungary we needed a rest break and so started looking for a place to stop. Aha! we spied a familiar sight, McDonald's! Yes they had just begun to spring up across Hungary and Romania. We stopped for a bite to eat and then set off again.

Our car was loaded with all sorts of things still much needed in Romania. We hadn't gone too far along the motorway when I was aware of a white car beside me signalling for us to stop, it gradually got closer until we were forced to stop on the hard shoulder beside the road. I immediately became suspicious, but Derek was trying to make out what they were saying. It appeared that they were trying to tell us that we had a problem with our back wheel.

This did seem to me to be quite unlikely as we had only had this car from new about two months before. However the car did seem to have wobbled a bit just before we stopped so Derek got out of the car to see what the man was trying to tell him.

I remember sitting praying that we would be kept safe. Derek and the man made their way to the back of the car and the man got down under the back where he said the problem was coming from the wheel.

He returned to his car and drove off and we decided that we would carry on driving very carefully until we could find somewhere to turn off and find a garage to check what our problem was.

We had driven slowly for twenty miles or so and found a slip road and just as we started to turn off discovered that we had a flat tyre!

We had to unload most of the things in the back of the car to get to the spare wheel. Derek had just about managed to change the wheel when I was aware that someone was standing beside him.

I got out to see what was happening as there seemed to be a bit of tugging going on and the man was saying that he was trying to help. Derek assured him that it was okay and that he had managed to change the wheel himself.

The man got in his car with another man who was with him and drove off. At that point Derek said to me "that was the man that stopped us before." When we got back in the car we realised that my bag had gone and so had Derek's video camera.   In my bag I had three thousand pounds!   It was money that we were taking to support a lovely family with their five children whose father had died.

We also had money to support another child named Alina who we had known since our first visit to the orphanage and it was to support her and her adoptive mother.

The rest of the money was for us to live on for the three months that we were to be there and also to support a few other smaller projects,. HOWEVER in another blue check canvas shopping bag I had fifteen thousand pounds in cash which was to pay for the extension work for a   Christian home for children that we had bought with our church. It was also to pay for the upkeep for the staff and children there! They hadn't found that!

With my bag gone so had our passports! I phoned home to get the locks changed on our house as my keys were there, and our address was in my bag too. We also phoned to ask folk at home to pray too.

We understood later that McDonald's was a familiar place where foreigners often stopped to eat. So criminals targeted people with GB number plates that looked as though they may be taking aid to Romania. Just past McDonald's the road became very uneven and so it was quite understandable to point out a defect on the car as it wobbled over that part of the road!

Now we had to find a police station to report what had happened..........

A lovely lady interpreter came who told us about something that had happened a few months earlier. A couple from England had been driving through Hungary to Romania and had stopped overnight near to where we had been stopped. Their camper van was broken into and the husband had been killed. The police caught the killers and they were in jail. What had impressed the interpreter was that this couple were Christians and the wife had returned just the week before this to go to the jail and meet her husband's killers and to tell them that she forgave them!

We managed to find somewhere to stay that night and the next day we had to go to the British Embassy to try to get our passports replaced. We then realised that we would not be able to get out of Hungary as we didn't have an entry visa in our passports and couldn't leave without one.

Another difficulty at the police station was because of the corruption it meant that if you didn't pay a bribe they were not very co-operative! However we did eventually get on our way again and although really shaken up by our experience (we found out that the man had put a spike in our tyre) . We were once again thankful for Gods protection on our lives.

ALINA, THE CONTINUING STORY

We returned home earlier than planned in November 1998 to start doing the home study. The social worker that had been assigned to us was a very understanding and kind lady who understood the need to do this as quickly as possible. The whole process was crammed into just three months and in February of 1999 we went to the panel and were approved as adoptive parents of Alina!

I then returned to Romania straight away whilst Derek had to wait in England for six weeks to get all of the legal paperwork done so that we could then get all the legal things done that we needed to in Romania.

Alina by this time was very poorly and in hospital, she didn't think we would keep our promise and come back for her! However on my return I managed to persuade the authorities that she would get better quicker if she could come and live with me in the apartment where I was staying and immediately her health began to improve.

When Derek arrived from England at the beginning of April with the papers, we then had to start the process of adoption in Romania. Not an easy thing to do and we spent many hours waiting for papers to be passed.

There were a lot of things that happened to try to stop the adoption going through and we saw many miracles during that time. We urgently needed to get Alina's original birth certificate and adoption papers from the Registry office in Focsani. It was Friday afternoon and we needed them to take to Bucuresti. We had an appointment at the British Embassy early on Monday morning and we needed to get the papers that afternoon to be able to get her visa to come to England. My faith dropped at that point, but Alina wasn't having it "lets pray anyway Mum and Dad" she said."I know we will be able to get it".

Pat and Derek with Alina the day they got the papers from the registry office in Focsani for her adoption

We arrived to find the offices closed for the day. Alina prayed again and at that moment a lady came to the door about to leave to go home. We explained our plight, and she took us inside and up to the office where she was able to give us the papers we needed. No money passed hands, no gift given over, it was God's answer to Alina's prayer of faith.

. But there was still one last obstacle......... to get her a visa from the

British Embassy. Especially as they had to interview Alina on her own to make sure that she wanted us to adopt her. However she came through the interview successfully which was quite an achievement considering that she chose to be interviewed in English.

Alina finally came to England as our daughter in May 1999 and one year later we had to adopt her again in the English court.

And so the next chapter of our lives began.......

THE 'KIDNAP'

As we turned in to the orphanage grounds one morning in 1997 we could see the children's faces pressed against the upstairs windows, looking out for us. What would we do with them today? Some games? Colouring? Singing? Maybe spend a little while outside in the grounds on this cold November day?

As they clambered around us we realised that one of our little friends was missing! Where was Edi? He had been very poorly when we saw him yesterday! "He's gone to the hospital" we were told.

We stayed for the morning and helped with the lunch, usually this was ciorba (pronounced chorba) a watery soup made with meat bones with a few vegetables and maybe a little piece of meat, also some bread. This was served in a little tin mug.....the bread just put on the table. Then it was time for the afternoon siesta when everything stopped, and everyone slept for the next few hours.

We usually went back to the apartment and had a rest ourselves before either returning to the orphanage or maybe visiting one of our friends. However on this particular day our thoughts were with Edi, our little friend who had been so poorly.

Hospitals in Romania at that time were bad, many had mixed rooms, with adults and children sharing the same room, sometimes patients even having to share a bed! But this one was called 'The Bad Hospital' by everyone (it was the infectious diseases hospital).

We wanted to see Edi for ourselves, and give him a little comfort. We had a little toy car to take to him and had managed to get a banana for him as well. We set off to the hospital which was some way out of the main part of town.

We were shown to the room where Edi was. There was a very sick lady there and another child in the room.

The windows were cracked and letting in the even colder air from outside. No curtains or blinds hung at the windows but some old bits of material had been stuffed into some of the cracked windows in an attempt to keep out the cold winds.

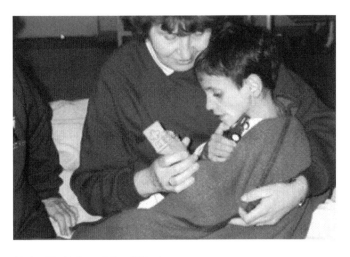

Pat with Edi and the little toy car

There was Edi, his little body no more than skin and bone, his big eyes sunken in their sockets, but as we reached him they lit up in recognition. He was tied to the bed, his arms and legs bound - we didn't understand why! He was covered with a blue grey threadbare blanket that wouldn't have given any warmth at all. At the bottom of the bed lay a candle. In Romanian Orthodox tradition you had to have a candle which was to be lit and put into your hands as you died, it would show the path to heaven. Nothing else mattered!

We untied Edi and gave him the banana, which he devoured hungrily. He sat on my lap for a cuddle, laying his head on my chest, we sang to him some English songs that we had taught the children and then some Romanian ones we had learned, then finished with Isus Hristos et Domnul (Jesus Christ is Lord) El vindeca bolnavii (He heals the sick).

We stayed for a while and Edi was as reluctant for us to leave him as we were to go. He pleaded with us to take him back to the orphanage, all he wanted was to be with his friends.

Feeling very sad we left him and made our way back to our apartment. At that time we were staying with Danut, the doctor who was the director of the orphanage.......a lovely caring man.

When we got there we told him how we had found Edi (he already knew of the state he would be in all on his own in that dreadful hospital}

"Please can we take him back to the orphanage so that he can be with his little friends?" we asked.

After much chat and persuasion Danut agreed that he would ask permission for us to take Edi back but he wouldn't be allowed to die in the orphanage!

The next morning we set off to the hospital to collect Edi. We had some new clothes with us that we had managed to keep back in case we may need them for such a child.

There were no staff to be seen anywhere so we made our way to the room where Edi lay. The ties were back on, the little car had disappeared. His big eyes looked up with just a glimmer of hope! Yes we told him, he could go home to the orphanage.

After waiting an hour or so and no staff appearing I went to see if I could find someone. There was nobody in the little staff room and no one to be seen anywhere I looked. So having permission (as we thought) from the orphanage director, that Edi could go back, we got him dressed and helped him out to our car. (We had driven there from England and had our own car with us).

We took our time returning, going past the park, then up past the main square just for a little drive.

We were met at the door by an anxious Danut and a few of the staff looking worried too.

It appeared that soon after our departure from the hospital it was discovered that Edi was missing. Had he been kidnapped?? Well yes I suppose he had!

Fortunately Danut was able to placate the hospital Director and stop her reporting us to the police.

Edi was pleased to be back with his friends and although weak he enjoyed watching the others in their activities.

****

Sadly Edi died three weeks later, and yes he did have to go back to the bad hospital.

I am sure that the candle was lit for him and placed in his hands there on his own, but I know that he wasn't alone, that Jesus WAS with him to welcome him to heaven!

COACH TRIP, BARBECUE AND WEDDINGS

It was Friday and a hot summer day. With the weekend ahead Danut thought it would be a good idea to go to Lepsa, a little village in the beautiful mountains above Focsani. It was about an hour and half drive up very steep hairpin bends, with a   couple of very small villages on the way up and a few little houses scattered near to the road.

Danut had been rushing around that afternoon and was extremely pleased to tell us to get ready as we were going to go to Lepsa. He had acquired a coach from somewhere (it looked really ancient). Some of the orphanage staff and several friends and family were coming too. We all set off to spend the weekend there. We were the only ones to take a change of clothes with us, others just got on the coach and went with what they had on!

We had been going for some forty-five minutes when there was a lot of commotion and everyone had to get off. The brakes on the coach had become red hot and were about to catch fire! The driver ran to the well by the side of the road and after pulling up many buckets of water to throw over the wheels and brakes it had cooled enough for us to continue on our way.

Danut was building a house there and that was to be where we would spend the weekend. However there was no running water and no well! So nothing to drink except wine or goats milk- ugh! In 30c plus heat that was not very comfortable.

There was dancing and singing that evening and when it came to time for bed we weren't quite sure how or where we would sleep as there didn't seem to be any bedrooms. Thankfully a neighbour offered for us to stay in their home so we had a bed, I think the rest of our party just slept on the floor or in the chairs.

The next morning they said we would have a barbecue - not quite like any that we had experienced in England.

First of all they had to cut down some wood from the trees, this being green wood which had to then be dried out and then burnt to make charcoal, the b a r b e c u e   w a s   e v e n t u a l l y ready...........late that afternoon, but it was delicious!.   The scenery was beautiful and we went for a walk to find a wonderful waterfall (cascada).

A typical village scene.

On another visit to Lepsa with Danut and his family we went by car.. Some way up the mountain we came across a policeman standing in the middle of the road waving us down.. He needed a lift up to the next village so that he could make a telephone call as a lorry had come off the road and plunged down the side of the mountain! I think it took until the next day to winch it up and rescue the driver, but we did understand that he was taken to hospital and survived.

****

We have been to several weddings during our time in Romania and each one has been different.

I think we were a bit of a novelty as we were invited to some that we didn't even know the couple getting married.

In Romania the bridegroom goes to collect the bride from her house and then there is a procession through the streets with singing and dancing, these have been the times that we have been invited to join them, although we never did.

Two weddings that stand out quite clearly in my mind were these, the first being at the Brethren church. It was a very solemn and sombre affair. The bride and groom sat on the platform at the front of the church while there seemed to be a lot of preaching and I don't remember the bride and groom taking part at all.

They had already been married in the civil wedding which made it legal. (Everyone has to have a civil wedding) but the church did not recognise this and so they didn't become man and wife in its eyes until after the church wedding.

In the church hall afterwards as we sat at one of the long tables, someone put a plate in front of me with about fifteen small cakes on it and then another plateful was put in front of Derek. We assumed that they were offering us some cake first as we were special guests, so we took one each and put the rest in the middle of the table, but no.........there was a plate for each person with as many cakes on it and we were supposed to eat them all!

The wedding that stays in my mind most was that of Oana and Gheorgita. We had known Gheorgita's family for a few years. They had already had the civil marriage and so were legally married, they also had a little baby boy. However they really wanted the traditional Romanian orthodox wedding, but couldn't afford it before. We had been able to let them have some money to help pay for this.

The day came and earlier on in the day the baby was to be baptised . In the orthodox church babies are baptised naked and fully immersed in water!

The wedding was due to take place at four that afternoon. We arrived at the apartment ready to follow the party to church, only to be met by the bridegroom pacing up and down outside as the priest who was to marry them was drunk and they had to find another one willing to take the wedding service!

The wedding itself was very different to the ones here in England. In the orthodox church you don't sit down although there are a few concrete seats built into the walls but not for many.

The bride and groom each had a crown put on their heads which then seemed to be swapped over each others heads several times.

There were also many icons in the church all over the walls, some high and some low. The bride and groom had to go and kiss them all!

With the ceremony over, off we went to the reception,. We sat down to the meal which by this time was almost at the end of the evening and I think it was about one in the morning when we realised that this was likely to go on for the rest of the night and into the next morning.

Then it was time for the giving of gifts. First the best man and the best woman were given a gift. On this occasion it was a carpet, rolled up and carried in and put on their shoulders. (We still don't understand the tradition of giving costly gifts to the best man and woman!)

After this each guest had to say what they were giving the bride and groom. This had to be money and as they said the amount given, the next person couldn't say less and lose face, so it either had to be the same or more. When we realised that we would have to say how much we had given we knew that it would make it very difficult for the people after us, and so decided at this point to make a move and return to our apartment

TOOTHPICKS AND MESSAGES

On one occasion we had come Romania to stay for three months. Many times before we had stayed with Danut the director of the orphanage, his wife Gabi and their little daughter Maria. But now we realised that we should be a little more independent.

We had asked the church if they could find an apartment that we could rent for a few months!   We arrived at the apartment complete with a few things that we thought might be necessary for our long stay.   Tanta greeted us and showed us around. It was the nicest apartment that I had seen in Romania with a bedroom, living room, a kitchen with a little table and a bathroom.

We unpacked our things and made ourselves at home, and it took quite a little while for us to realise that we hadn't actually rented the apartment and that Tanta and Madalina would be living there with us!

Tanta was a lady in her early thirties, Madalina her daughter was four years old. Six months before we arrived Tanta's husband Mitica had gone out to play football when he had a heart attack and died and never returned home.

Tanta had hardly left her bed since then until we arrived. Although we had hoped to be on our own in the apartment, God always goes before us and knows what is better! Over the coming months we became really good friends, the language barrier broken with laughter as we realised the fun we had trying to translate each other languages. Sometime this was done with the help of reading both the English and Romanian bibles.

One funny thing that I remember was when there was a pack of toothpicks on the table. Tanta looked at them then at us and said "toothpick English" after some wondering we realised she thought she was saying "do you speak English"!!

Tanta was to become a great friend who we love dearly, she came to England for three months that year for a holiday with Alina. She had hoped to be able to work in England as she had no income since Mitica died, however we hoped that the three months in England would help her in her grief for her husband.

One day soon after we came to the apartment we had just got home when Tanta told us that there was a lady from the church that wanted to see us as she had a 'message' for us.

We were very tired and didn't really want to go and listen to what we thought might be a very long message.

Well we knew that we would have to in the end, so reluctantly we went to meet her. It turned out that it was not a message but a massage that she wanted to give us, and before we realised it Derek was on the bed with just his pants on whilst she proceeded to give the massage!

This lady was blind and her job was as a physiotherapist at the hospital and we were invited along to see her at work.

The hospital area that she was working in was very sparse. There was one of her patients on a bed and she had a little table at the end of the bed where she sat us with some home made beer! She then decided that it was my turn for the massage, only this time it was an electric pulse machine. Well that may have been ok, but when I saw the ancient machine with bare electric wires, I decided to opt out, especially when she got close to my leg that had metal pins in it!

THE 'STALKER'

D on't worry - I know the way". These were my parting words to Derek as I set out early one afternoon to see a friend - a lady doctor from the orphanage we were working in.

Derek didn't want to come with me for a girly chat, and like most Romanians in the afternoon, opted for a sleep. The whole town slept, shops shut, schools shut, no one would be about.

It was quite a long walk from our apartment to Paula's, about forty five minutes by the route I usually took. Straight up our road to the main street into town, past the orphanage then straight on until you reach the train station then turn left. Str Longinescu was a long road and the block I was visiting was right at the far end.

If I was right I should be able to cut about twenty minutes from my walk by weaving between the blocks.

So off I set. I was soon aware that I was being followed and by a man in a military officers uniform.   Each time I turned he turned and kept the same distance behind me.

My heart was racing as I imagined being taken away for questioning! This was very soon after the revolution and the fear from the people was tangible. Neighbours spied on neighbours and reported them to the Securitate, everyone was suspicious, even sometimes of their own family.

Well eventually I reached the block, yes I'm sure this is the right block number! I turned in to the entrance - my follower turned in too……..

Up three flights of stairs he followed me. As I stood trembling and knocking at my friends door, my follower said something to me that I didn't understand. The little boy that opened the door didn't belong to my friend and seemed quite pleased to see the man beside me. I told him my friend's name and the man indicated it was the floor above!

Now was that a coincidence? Did I just learn a little bit more of what life must have felt like there in communist times?

Perhaps it was that God showed me that even when I tried to rely on myself to do something, He would show me the better way! If I hadn't been followed and the man hadn't been there at that time I would never have found the right apartment.

KARISMA

In 1995 on our way through the country we visited a Christian orphanage and saw the great difference and the love the people had for the children there. We felt that perhaps God was calling us to set up a Christian orphanage and in 1996 we went specifically to see when, what and how this should come about. We hoped that we might find the possibility to work in Focsani with the children that we had come to love, but could not at that time find any Christians in that place that could help with a project like that.

However we were also involved with a Bible school in Sibiu some 150 miles west of Focsani, and through them found eight possibilities, but one of them seemed to be the right one and some Christian people that we knew and trusted were able to help us with the purchase and oversee the project. We knew that God was in the purchase of the house in Lancram, in mid Romania and we purchased it in June that year; in July the first eight children came to live there. We also knew a Christian couple who ran this for us and four other staff that worked there too.

This grew to fifteen children between the ages of five and sixteen. The father of the children next door had died the year before and the mother being a very poor lady could not afford to keep them and so they were going to a state orphanage, but they were able to stay with her and come into our home (Karisma) during the day for meals, and also to have help with clothing and their school work.

Outside Karism

It was a great place with a sense of God's presence there. Our home church in England, Thundersley Congregational Church, gladly supported the work and a number of people were able to go out there to visit. We extended the buildings, and the cost of running the place for the next few years was about

£1000 per month, but God was good in supplying all the needs at that time.
Outside Karisma

Tanta and Madalina had by this time gone to live and work in Rome and Derek and I were living at her apartment by ourselves.

The Pastor of our Church, Dave and his wife Alice had come out to visit us to see for themselves the orphanage and also to go with us to visit Karisma our children's home in Lancram.

One morning Derek had gone to have a bath. The little window above the bath was very thick wood and glass that was meant to help insulate for the very cold winters there. The corners were very sharp and as Derek stood up he cracked his head on the window slicing it open.

The groaning sound he made was awful as he staggered back into the bedroom without a stitch of clothing on. Blood was pouring from his head and in a bit of a panic I called for Alice to come and help me.

Well I hadn't realised that Alice had a bit of a blood phobia and when she saw the state of Derek's head she fainted! Oh dear! Now two casualties instead of one! Well Alice revived okay and I manage to get her back to the living room where they were sleeping. Fortunately I had come laden with all sorts of things I may need so out came the Steristrips and I managed to close up the hole in Derek's head.

We then went across country to Karisma which was several hours drive through the mountains. I just wanted to say here that I was very proud of Alice as while we were at Karisma NIcu, one of the Karisma kids sliced his leg open from his thigh to his knee. The hospital was a long way away, but this time Alice overcame the sight of all the blood and managed to hold Nicu's leg wound together whilst I once again applied my steristrips! I think I used up the entire supply on his leg. I'm pleased to say that his leg healed well and that he didn't need to go to the hospital

HOME OF HOPE

Although we had bought and started Karisma, our children's home in Lancram our hearts were still with the children that we had first met in Focsani and we still spent much of our time there with them..

Evelyn, with whom we had first gone to Romania in 1990 with the YWAM team and another lady called Ruth had met a lovely young married couple called Hajnal and Florin, who were willing to be house parents if it was possible to buy and start a home in Focsani.

As we had already done all of the legal process for Karisma, Evelyn and Ruth asked how we had done this and how they might be able to set up a similar project in Focsani. They had found a house which was in need of a great deal of renovation, it was made into two apartments with another young couple parenting the children upstairs.

So on Christmas Eve 1999 twelve of the children (who by this time were about twelve years old) came from orphanage two to live at Casa Sperantei - Home of Hope.

I know there have been heartaches and joys for them all at this place, but it is a wonderful place full of love and Gods grace and blessings where some of the children who are now adults still live, and have found a mum and dad that love them, and also have found that wonderful love of God for themselves.

SNOW SLIDES AND A
HEADLESS COW!

In 1996 in England I had fallen off a ladder and broken my ankle and tibia. I had to have an operation and have pins and plates inserted in my leg and ankle before it was put in plaster; this was just three weeks before we were due to return to Romania. At the airport it was hard to make them understand that I was not trying to smuggle something inside the plaster on my leg. They took my crutches away and then asked me to walk through the X-ray arch. I said that I couldn't walk without the crutches and they tugged at my plaster to see if I was hiding anything down there.

When we arrived in Romania it was very difficult as we had to travel across the country by train. The trains there are very high up from the platform (or rather the platforms were very low!). So I had to climb up the steps into the carriage, difficult with a plastered leg. It was November and a very cold winter. As we travelled we had to get towels out of our luggage to try to warm ourselves up a little bit, and put plastic bags over my foot to keep it dry.

On one of our visits when we were buying the house in Lancram we had been staying at the Bible school in Sibiu but had gone to the village where we had been invited to stay at the pastor's house. We had gone by minibus from the Bible school and whilst in the village they had bought a cow to take back to be slaughtered and the meat used to feed the students and staff at the Bible school.

The only thing was that they had intended to take the cow back alive in the minibus but when they tried to get the cow into the mini bus it was too big and so they had killed it and cut off its head. The head was given to the pastor who was very pleased with this gift and insisted that 'we will be having some of the head for a meal this evening' It would probably feed the family there for the rest of the month too We decided at that point that we perhaps would return to the Bible school that night after all!.

The winter time was extremely cold. The snow was very deep and the all the town children loved to make slides on the paths . Wherever you walked the snow was very deep and was compacted on the pavements. Children had made snow slides everywhere and you had to be extremely careful that you didn't step onto one. We had been out visiting friends one evening and then were walking back late at night in the dark to our apartment. We had to be very careful as we walked home watching how and where we put our feet so as not to step onto the slides.

Just as we got outside of our apartment I looked up at the window to see if the light was on to know if Tanta would be in, but as I did so I stepped on the slide outside and fell backwards, and cracked my head on the ground. Just then another lady walked past me and looking down at me also stepped on the slide and fell next to me on the pavement.......

My head felt really painful but I didn't want to go to the hospital although I might have done had I been in England. We decided that we would just pray and perhaps have a game of Upwords to keep me alert as I really felt that I may had done some damage and didn't think it was a good idea to fall asleep! Another answer to prayer as I felt fine the next day apart from being a bit shaken up and quite tired from our sleepless night.

One of the really nice things about the winter and the deep snow was being able to take the children outside to make snowmen and snow angels, they loved it!!

I had taken a few different items of food with us from England that I knew I would not be able to find in the shops there. One of them being strawberry jelly. I had managed to get a tin of pineapple from a shop and made a jelly with pineapple in it and left it on the cold balcony to set while we were out. On my return I went to get the jelly from the balcony and wondered if perhaps you could get jellies in Romania after all as this now was not a red jelly but a yellow one. But of course it was the acid in the pineapple that was taking the colour out of the strawberry jelly!

LOCAL TV APPEARANCE

Our main mission was to work alongside the children in the orphanages but we also brought out several teams from our church in Thundersley to work with the churches doing street mission work and visiting some of the village churches.

As Romania had been under communist rule for so many years, many people were eager to hear of the Christian faith; when asked why they would listen to us we were told it was because of our Christian heritage in England.

The people were hungry to hear the word of God and for Bibles and any Christian literature. There was some fighting to get hold of tracts which we offered when we visited some of the villages.

We also were expected to speak in the churches (well the men were; ladies didn't speak in the churches at that time) and to bring greetings from

Handing out tracts in a village

our church in England. One of our team who had only become a Christian on our first visit to Romania was asked to speak on Philadelphia, and he asked if they meant the cheese!

Derek spoke a few times and the group were also asked to sing. Derek had a beautiful singing voice and was able to harmonise so I think together we managed to sound reasonably good!

The local television company had heard about our visit there and so the team was asked to do a half hour tv programme. We did some sketches that we had learnt in Romanian, singing, and bringing inspiring stories that were translated for us.

ARMED ROBBERY

Back in England on a cold New Years eve, there was much to be done before the evening when we hoped to get to the church party and then the Watch night service to see the new year in.

If I hurried I could get the shopping that I needed and still get to the travel agents before they closed. I needed to book our flights to Romania, this time going for three months! As the travel company charged for using credit cards I decided to draw out the cash to pay for our tickets.

The shopping precinct was very busy with people buying at the sales. I pushed open the door to the travel agents hoping that there wouldn't be many people ahead of me. One other couple were being attended to and another man on his own, but the first agent as I got inside the door was free. I sat down and proceeded to book our flights.

The booking complete I got the cash out of my bag and was just about to hand it over, when suddenly the door burst open and two gunmen in balaclavas burst through the door! One man sat down on a chair about two feet away from me with his gun pointed straight at me! The other man pushed the staff through to the back asking for money from the safe. I could feel the gunman's eyes boring into me - the gun levelled at my head. And there I sat with £500 in my hands for anyone to see!

"Lord please keep us safe", I prayed, "I don't mind if they take the money just keep us safe!"

It seemed as though there was an invisible shield and the man couldn't see the money, and gradually I managed to tuck it out of sight.

For what seemed like ages we sat there; another couple came in, commented on the lack of staff and went out again! Then another customer came in and started to look at the brochures.

Just then the gunman came from the back, smacked the customer seated nearest to him round the head with the gun and then the pair ran off and disappeared into the crowded shopping precinct.

The staff rushed out and locked the doors, the astonished customer who was browsing the brochures hadn't realised he'd been in on an armed robbery!

All the staff were in a state of shock and there was a lot of crying. I went out to the staff area at the back and made them all a cup of tea whilst we waited for the police, surprised at how calm I was and thanking God for keeping us all safe that day!

Yes, I did get to the church party with Derek that evening and then to see the new year in thanking God again for another time of protection in my life.

COW-WALKING CAR MECHANIC!

In Romania yet again we had borrowed a very old car to travel on a three hundred mile round trip across the mountains to Lancram to visit and oversee the work on Karisma. The brakes were very dodgy and we had to learn very quickly not to rely on them on the steep hairpin bends through some of the mountain passes, but slow down by changing to very low gear. A hair-raising experience!

We were travelling through a very isolated part with no sign of habitation for miles and we ground to a halt. Derek looked under the bonnet and although he had some idea of car mechanics this completely baffled him.

We sent up a little arrow prayer. "Well Lord, we really need you to get us out of this fix but we have no idea how you are going to do it". So we sat in the car and calmly waited for an answer.

After a few minutes an elderly man came along the road walking his cow; it was not unusual to see cows being walked from place to place to give them exercise and find pasture.

He realised straight away that we were in trouble, then told us that he was a car mechanic and he had a little garage set back behind some trees just a little further up the road! He had just the part we needed and was able to fix the car so we could be on our way again.

Thank you once again Lord and another lesson in trusting.

TRAVELLING ANECDOTES

On our first visit by road we had just crossed over the border into Romania and were not quite sure what to expect. The country had a different feel to it like travelling back in time to a former age! We came to a very small village with some of the villagers sitting outside their homes and chickens and small animals running on the road. Unfortunately as we drove through the village we managed to hit one or two chickens and left the poor villagers stunned and staring in amazement as we carried on through, not wanting to stop and face the wrath of folk that we didn't know the language to communicate with!

The village transport in those days was mainly by horse and cart or sometimes even bullock carts.

On another occasion whilst travelling through a village (probably going too fast) we managed to spook a horse and cart and it careered off down the road with the poor man hanging on for dear life. As he disappeared into the distance the scene reminded me of something from a wild western film!

I felt we did not give a very good impression of Westerners.......

****

On our early travels across Europe and then across Romania we used to take cans of diesel with us as there were constant shortages of petrol and diesel. Queues for fuel were seen at every garage and sometimes people queued for days on end along the roads to wait for deliveries of fuel. When it arrived they would push the cars along the queue to save fuel.

On one occasion as we were returning through Romania on our way home on an extremely hot day we came across a blockade in the road with many angry men stopping the traffic going through as they were not able to get fuel.

We felt very uncomfortable as we thought the situation could turn nasty and kept our windows closed although the temperature outside and inside was almost unbearable; in the back or our trailer we had several gallons of diesel. We always took fuel with us to enable us to get out of Romania if we were unable to buy any there.

****

Ahead of us we could see a long queue of stationary cars and lorries and we slowed to a stop on the autobahn in Germany.

The roads were some of the best on our journey across Europe and we relied on these good roads in the timings to reach our overnight stops.

We had travelled this route many times before and now were wondering what the cause may be for what turned out to be quite a long delay…….some kind of accident?   Hopefully no one badly injured or killed, but we waited not knowing the reason.

People were getting out of their cars and chatting to one another, obviously this was going to be a long wait, but why?

After some time a police car with loud speaker came along the hard shoulder announcing to everyone the cause for the delay! An unexploded English wartime bomb! Oh dear, how embarrassing, we thought, as we stood in front of our GB number plates hoping that we might just be able to hide them.....

****

A lady was standing beside her car franticly waving at the passing traffic, smoke and flames coming out from under her car bonnet.

We were travelling in a convoy of three vehicles. We all pulled over and each of us rushed to get out our fire extinguishers and ran to put out the fire. We were in Hungary and the lady had been travelling alone and was on her way home to Germany. We stayed with her until she managed to contact her husband and he arranged for help to get her home.

****

"Any drugs or guns?" asked the border guard as we waited once again at the border into Hungary. The queues at the borders were always long and tedious at that time, and we waited sometimes for hours, for our papers so that we could get through. The corruption was bad and the wait was long if you didn't bribe. On one occasion the guard checking asked if we had any 'girly' magazines. I offered him my Womans' Own magazine! He took it and went off happily to bring us our papers and lift the barricade to let us through. I wondered what he might make of that - I don't think it was quite what he had expected!.

****

We sat in the dreary and depressing waiting room hoping that we would get our papers to pass through the border into Hungary before much longer.

There was so much corruption and it seemed to be the accepted thing that to get through the borders without too much delay would be costly but we didn't want to be part of that, and so stood firm and believed that God would get us through.

Many others had entered the room and collected their papers as a little packet was pushed towards the counter clerk.

My thoughts and prayers turned God-wards again, and at that moment a man entered the room, his presence seemed to fill the space   By his accent I think he was Dutch. He had a big bushy ginger beard and thick hair with a wonderful smile on his face.   As he walked in he started to sing in English 'How Great Thou Art'. His voice was deep and the singing was beautiful - I can still hear his voice in my head to this day.

He handed his papers over and they were stamped and returned to him straight away.

It seemed that as he had started to sing there was a shift in the atmosphere in the room. It almost felt as though a bright light had been switched on; it certainly seemed to be a lot brighter.

The lady behind the desk smiled at us and beckoned us over. The papers now stamped were passed back to us. We could be on our way again.

Thank you Lord for once again reminding me to put my trust in You.

****

We were travelling along the one and only motorway in Romania, fast traffic moving towards us on our side of the road! There was no central reservation and no restrictions of who could use it either

Just ahead of us on the left grass verge we saw a peasant lady running very fast, scarf flying, hands up in horror. Whatever was causing her to panic like that? We soon spotted the culprit was her runaway cow. Long rope that would usually be held firmly by the lady was trailing behind.

Thoughts flashed through my head, oh no, if the cow was to divert across the motorway we would be coming to a very sticky end.

No sooner had the thought come into my head than I saw the cow turn towards the motorway and an arrow prayer went up, which was really just 'Help please'...... The cow shot across right in front of us missing our car by inches and we ran over the trailing rope. The cow then disappeared across a field on our right. The 'help please' prayer turned into a 'Thank you Lord' and a big sigh of relief.

****

ALINA'S POEMS

We first met Alina in 1994. She was born in Bucuresti in 1986 and abandoned at birth in the hospital there, and so spent her first two years of life in an orphanage in that city.

When she was two years old her grandmother came to get her and take her home to live with her. She lived with her grandmother, her aunt and uncle and cousins for the next six years.

Alina on the day she arrived in the orphanage in Focsani

When she was eight her grandmother could no longer manage to look after her and so she took her to the orphanage in Focsani, a very sad and lonely little girl, which was when we first met her.

****

Here are some of the poems she wrote while in the orphanage at Focsani, originally in Romanian and here translated into English……

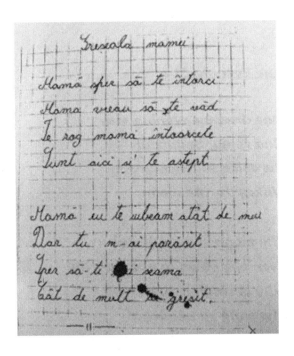

Mamas Mistake

Mama, I hope you will return
Mama,I want to see you
Please Mama come back
I am waiting for you
Mama I did love you very much
But you left me alone

I hope you understand what you have done
How big a mistake you made.

****

Mama
Mama, I want you to be with me
To tell me bedtime stories at night
Or whisper to tell me that you love me
These words would mean so much to
me

People are very much like cloth
They tear into threads
And the people their days

****

Somebody Better
From far away I can see some tears
They are tears held back for ages
When you miss your parents who you
did not know
That they can hurt you very much

The heart of a child left in a crowd of people
Being brought up by some woman's pity.
Who knows what that means - to be left in a crowd?
Not letting a tear come from her eye to her cheek
But it is still coming in the little girl's heart
Which one day she will begin to understand
What it means not to have had parents love
Or maybe she will, but from someone else

****

The Most Important Wishes

1 To be home with Granny again
2 To see my mother in person
3 To get well

The Less Important

4 I would like a keyboard
5 I would like a plastic doll with blue eyes
6 A big big teddy bear
7 A leather jacket

Who Can Help Me?

1 and 2 To convince Granny to give us her address and take me home. I would be very happy
3 Only God can help me
4 5 6 and 7 The English can resolve them

****

I wrote this book as a dedication to my beloved husband Derek, who went to be with His Saviour Jesus on 18th July 2020.

He has been my inspiration over the years as we shared the adventures in this book.

So as the book starts with the memories of a child in the orphanage dreaming of 'another day called tomorrow' - I now begin another chapter of my life, without Derek by my side, but wondering what 'another day called tomorrow' will bring for me? Another day - without Derek, but with God by my side still……….

If you would like to contact me about anything relating to this book, or would like to get to know Jesus and the God that I know email me at <ins>anotherday24@outlook.com</ins>

ACKNOWLEDGEMENT

WITH GRATEFUL THANKS TO MY SISTER JOYCE
WHITE (AUTHOR OF GOLD IN THE RIVER) WHO
ENCOURAGED ME TO WRITE DOWN THE
MEMORIES SHARED IN THIS BOOK

ALSO FOR ALL THE WORK SHE HAS DONE TO
HELP ME TO EDIT AND GET THIS BOOK
PUBLISHED

Printed in Great Britain
by Amazon